CORNERSTONES OF FREEDOM™

THE VIETNAM WAR

BY PETER BENOIT

CHILDREN'S PRESS®
An Imprint of Scholastic Inc.
New York   Toronto   London   Auckland   Sydney
Mexico City   New Delhi   Hong Kong
Danbury, Connecticut

BRINGING HISTORY to LIFE

Content Consultant
James Marten, PhD
Professor and Chair, History Department
Marquette University
Milwaukee, Wisconsin

Library of Congress Cataloging-in-Publication Data

Benoit, Peter, 1955–
  The Vietnam War / by Peter Benoit.
    p. cm.—(Cornerstones of freedom)
  Includes bibliographical references and index.
  ISBN 978-0-531-23608-6 (lib. bdg.) —ISBN 978-0-531-21966-9 (pbk.)
1. Vietnam War, 1961–1975—Juvenile literature. 2. Vietnam
War, 1961–1975—United States—Juvenile literature. I. Title.
  DS557.7.B46 2012
  959.704'3—dc23   2012034326

SCHOLASTIC, CHILDREN'S PRESS, CORNERSTONES OF FREEDOM™,
and associated logos are trademarks and/or registered trademarks of
Scholastic Inc.

1 2 3 4 5 6 7 8 9 10 R 22 21 20 19 18 17 16 15 14 13

Photographs © 2013: Alamy Images/Keystone Pictures USA: 32; AP
Images: 40 (Al Chang), 17 (Frank Waters), 5 top, 44 (Godfrey), 23 (Horst
Faas), 4 bottom, 19 (Le Minh), 24 (Malcolm Browne), 42, 57 (Rick Merron),
55 (USAID, Richard Nyberg), cover, 4 top, 12, 18, 22, 26, 34, 36, 46, 56 top;
Corbis Images: 14, 38, 50 (Bettmann), 39 (Hulton-Deutsch Collection), 47
(Wally McNamee), 43 (Yoichi Okamoto); Everett Collection: 35, 45; Getty
Images: 51 (Dirck Halstead), 15 (Gerard Fouet/AFP), 37 (Hulton Archive),
48 (John Filo), 16 (Keystone), back cover (Larry Burrows/Time & Life
Pictures), 5 bottom, 11, 30 (Universal Images Group); Library of Congress:
10 (Chase-Statler, Washington), 25 (New York World-Telegram and the
Sun Newspaper Photograph Collection/United Press International);
National Archives and Records Administration/White House Photo: 27
(ARC Identifier 192482), 28, 56 bottom (ARC Identifier 192484); The Granger
Collection: 8 (Rue des Archives), 6 (ullstein bild); The Image Works: 54
(Lynne Fernandes), 2, 3, 13, 20 (TopFoto).

Maps by XNR Productions, Inc.

Did you know that studying history can be fun?

BRING HISTORY TO LIFE by becoming a history investigator. Examine the evidence (primary and secondary source materials); cross-examine the people and witnesses. Take a look at what was happening at the time—but be careful! What happened years ago might suddenly become incredibly interesting and change the way you think!

Contents

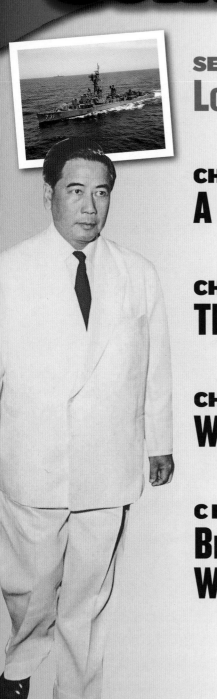

4

Long Time Coming

The French military took over Vietnam in the late 19th century.

The Vietnam War was one of the most devastating events of the 20th century. Hundreds of thousands of people died during combat. Differing opinions on the war caused huge divisions in American society.

EUROPEANS FIRST SETTLED IN

The seeds of the Vietnam War were sown long before its start. By the mid-1880s, France had forcefully colonized all of Vietnam. It became part of a large French colony known as Indochina. The colony also included modern-day Laos and Cambodia. France made huge amounts of money growing crops in Indochina to sell to Europe. But the Vietnamese people became increasingly frustrated by colonial rule. A number of **nationalist** groups fought against France for self-government. France defeated all resistance and maintained control until World War II (1939–1945).

After German forces invaded France in 1940, control of Vietnam passed to Japan, an ally of Germany. By 1945, Vietnamese nationalist groups had become active once again. One group was called the Viet Minh. It was led by the Soviet-trained **communist** Ho Chi Minh. The United States supported Ho's efforts to force Japanese troops out of Vietnam. As a result, the Viet Minh controlled much of northern Vietnam before the end of the war. But the French were able to regain military control in Vietnam after the war ended in 1945. Seeing their gains reversed, the Viet Minh attacked a French patrol boat in Haiphong Harbor. The French struck back against the Viet Minh at Haiphong on November 23, 1946. The conflict presented U.S. president Harry Truman with a difficult choice. His decision would forever alter the course of American history.

VIETNAM IN THE 16TH CENTURY.

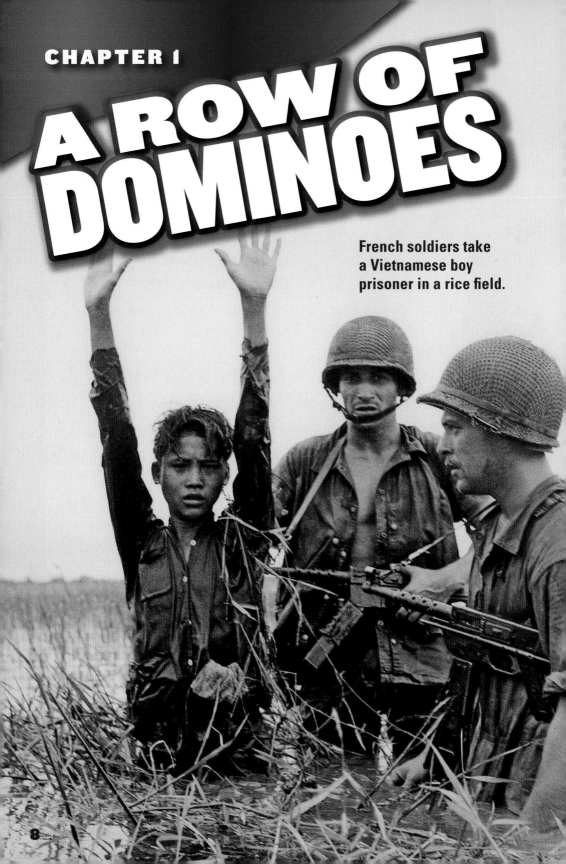

CHAPTER 1

A ROW OF DOMINOES

French soldiers take a Vietnamese boy prisoner in a rice field.

PRESIDENT TRUMAN WAS

opposed to the idea of countries such as France taking over and controlling large parts of the world. But he also feared that Ho Chi Minh would spread his communist beliefs throughout Southeast Asia if the United States supported the Viet Minh. Truman was faced with a choice between supporting France's efforts to control Vietnam and allowing communism to expand. He decided to side with France. Despite failing to win support from the United States, Ho Chi Minh was certain that colonialism was dying out. He did not think the French forces could defeat his Viet Minh army.

President Truman wanted to prevent communist influence from spreading throughout the world.

The Spread of Communism

Truman recognized that trade among the United States, Western Europe, and Southeast Asian colonies would speed Europe's **economic** recovery from World War II. He also incorrectly assumed that Ho was acting in agreement with the Soviet Union. The Soviet Union was a communist nation that had become a powerful rival of the United States in the aftermath of the war. The Soviets were rapidly expanding into neighboring areas. The United States responded by developing a policy of slowing or stopping this expansion as much as possible. This policy was known as containment.

Truman feared that giving support to Ho would lead to Soviet control of strategic water routes connecting the Pacific Ocean and the Middle East. This would go against the containment policy. Truman also knew that France would be a valuable ally in any struggles against the Soviets.

In August 1949, the Soviets proved with a test explosion that they had successfully created an atomic bomb. The United States was no longer the only nation to possess this powerful weapon. That same year, communists achieved victory in a civil war in China. Communists were gaining more power around the world. Truman decided to contain the spread of communism at all costs. Congress responded to these developments by sending military aid to the French.

Soviet nuclear weapons were a major concern for U.S. leaders.

Chaos in Asia

In June 1950, North Korean prime minister Kim Il-Sung sent 100,000 troops into South Korea with Soviet approval. U.S. general Douglas MacArthur drove the communist North Korean forces back. But his aggressive strategy brought 200,000 Chinese troops to Kim's aid. This raised the possibility of similar Chinese involvement in Vietnam. In August, Truman sent a small group of military advisers to Saigon, the Vietnamese capital, to help train Vietnamese troops who were fighting with France against the Viet Minh. By 1952, the United States was financing one-third of France's war in Vietnam. But even this support did not keep the French forces from being pushed back.

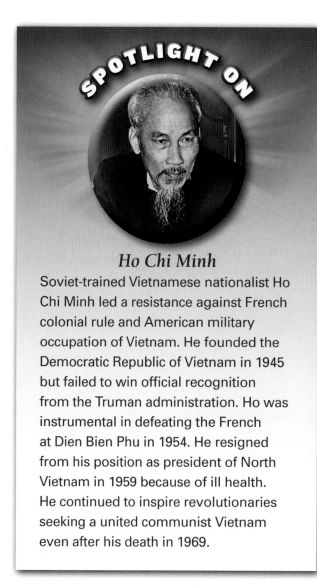

SPOTLIGHT ON

Ho Chi Minh

Soviet-trained Vietnamese nationalist Ho Chi Minh led a resistance against French colonial rule and American military occupation of Vietnam. He founded the Democratic Republic of Vietnam in 1945 but failed to win official recognition from the Truman administration. Ho was instrumental in defeating the French at Dien Bien Phu in 1954. He resigned from his position as president of North Vietnam in 1959 because of ill health. He continued to inspire revolutionaries seeking a united communist Vietnam even after his death in 1969.

The French military suffered heavy losses in its conflict with Vietnam.

France's position had worsened further by April 1953. The Viet Minh expanded operations deep into the Tonkin region in the northern portion of Vietnam. They also expanded westward into the neighboring country of Laos.

France's Failure

France was alarmed by the expansion of the Viet Minh. Its leaders asked U.S. president Dwight Eisenhower for help airlifting heavy equipment into Laos. They hoped to disrupt the rear of the Viet Minh advance by cutting supply lines and blocking reinforcements. Eisenhower permitted Air Force ground personnel to assist but did not involve pilots in combat missions.

General Henri Navarre's occupation of Dien Bien Phu led to France's defeat in its struggle to control Vietnam.

In late 1953, French general Henri Navarre prepared to occupy the town of Dien Bien Phu in northwestern Vietnam. France hoped that taking the town would cut off important supply routes for the Viet Minh. Navarre and his men successfully took control of Dien Bien Phu. But they soon became trapped when Ho's forces cut off all of the roads leading into the town. Eisenhower briefly considered sending combat forces to assist Navarre but decided against military involvement. To send combat forces would amount to a declaration of war on North Vietnam.

On March 13, 1954, Viet Minh general Vo Nguyen Giap launched a vicious attack against the French forces in Dien Bien Phu. The battle raged back and forth until French bombers inflicted major losses on the Viet Minh on April 5. The fight then settled into a prolonged **siege**.

On May 7, Viet Minh forces began a final assault on the badly outnumbered French resistance in Dien Bien Phu. They won in a matter of hours and took nearly 12,000 prisoners in the process. France's rule in Vietnam had come to an end.

The Geneva Conference

Ten days before the Viet Minh victory, representatives from several nations met in Geneva, Switzerland,

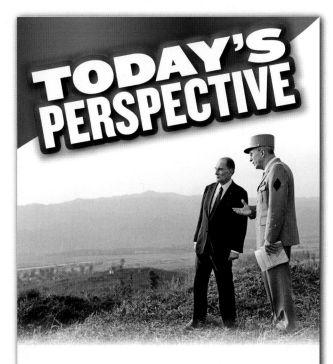

TODAY'S PERSPECTIVE

French president François Mitterrand (left) visited the site of the Battle of Dien Bien Phu in 1993. It was nearly four decades after the famous conflict. Mitterrand's presence enraged some Vietnamese who were not ready to forget the violence caused by French colonizers. Wounds have since begun to heal. French schools have been established in Hanoi, and French businesses have reached out to forge links with Vietnam.

At the Geneva Conference, leaders from around the world discussed ways to deal with the situation in Vietnam peacefully and fairly.

to discuss possibilities of peace in Indochina. The United States, China, France, and the Soviet Union all participated. So did leaders from both the Viet Minh and the southern Vietnamese, who supported the French military. After its defeat at Dien Bien Phu, France agreed to remove its troops from the region. The representatives then began making plans to **unify** Vietnam. An agreement was reached on July 21. Vietnam was temporarily divided into the nations of North Vietnam and South Vietnam. An election to unify the two separate nations was set for 1956.

A FIRSTHAND LOOK AT

THE FINAL DECLARATION OF THE GENEVA CONFERENCE

The Geneva Conference divided Vietnam into two separate nations. It also worked to end hostilities in Cambodia and Laos. See page 60 for a link to read the conference's Final Declaration online.

Supporting the South

U.S. leaders were nervous about the planned election. They were certain that Ho Chi Minh would win and begin to extend communism throughout Southeast Asia. To prevent this, they began supporting South Vietnam's anticommunist leader, Ngo Dinh Diem. They worked

U.S. leaders supported Ngo Dinh Diem (waving) because of his anticommunist policies.

with Diem to establish a stable government in South Vietnam. Acting against the terms established in Geneva, President Eisenhower provided an increasingly large number of U.S. military advisers to South Vietnam.

The United States also worked to make South Vietnam stronger by increasing its population. Vietnamese people could travel freely between the north and south nations during the three months following the Geneva Conference. The U.S. Navy transported more than 300,000 North Vietnamese civilians and soldiers to South Vietnam during this time. This was done in large part to increase support for Diem's leadership. Diem was a follower of Catholicism. Most of the Vietnamese moving from the north were also Catholic. But around 80 percent of the South Vietnamese population was Buddhist.

President Eisenhower (left) soon developed a close working relationship with Diem (right).

Diem's strong support of Catholicism made him unpopular among South Vietnam's Buddhist population.

Diem favored the Catholics and treated the large Buddhist majority unfairly. Catholics were routinely offered military promotions, tax breaks, and other advantages. This caused many South Vietnamese people to become unhappy with Diem's leadership.

Diem refused to participate when it came time to hold the unification election in 1956. He instead declared himself president of Vietnam. The United States continued to provide resources and help train the South Vietnamese military, even as people throughout Vietnam grew more and more frustrated with the situation.

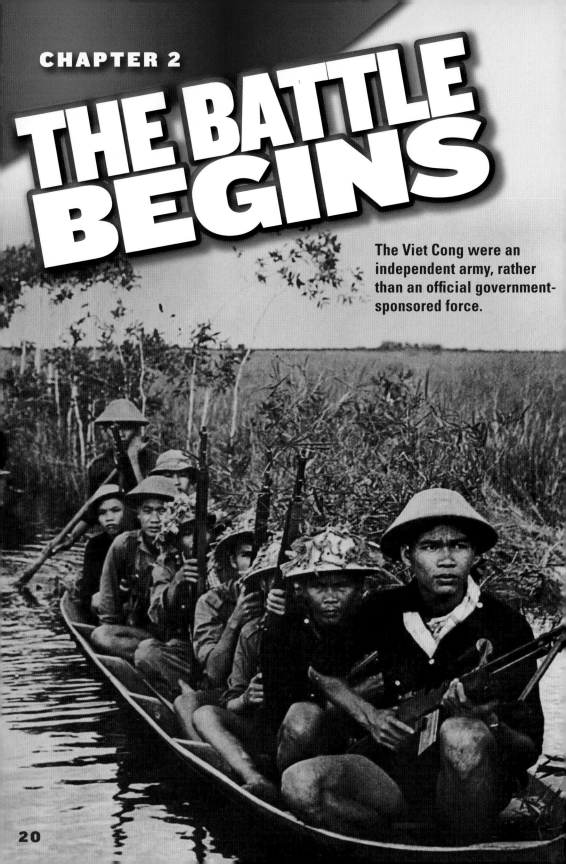

CHAPTER 2

THE BATTLE BEGINS

The Viet Cong were an independent army, rather than an official government-sponsored force.

SOON AFTER DIEM DECLARED himself president, North Vietnamese **insurgents** began launching raids and surprise attacks across the border into South Vietnam. These communist fighters called themselves the Viet Cong. Their numbers grew as more Vietnamese became unhappy with Diem's corrupt government. Many South Vietnamese people joined them. This weakened Diem's hold on the nation even more. The Viet Cong ambushed two South Vietnamese Army (ARVN) companies southwest of Saigon in September 1959. President Eisenhower responded by increasing the number of U.S. military advisers in South Vietnam to 685 men.

President John F. Kennedy continued U.S. support of Diem's South Vietnamese government.

Unofficially Involved

By the time U.S. president John F. Kennedy was sworn into office in January 1961, insurgents threatened the survival of the South Vietnamese government. Kennedy responded by sending U.S. Army Special Forces and Air Force advisers to train South Vietnamese pilots. These advisers also flew secret missions in support of ARVN ground forces. The United States had finally taken an active role in the conflict.

By October 1961, President Kennedy was faced with a major decision. He sent two advisers to Vietnam to determine South Vietnam's chances of defeating the Viet Cong without assistance. Both agreed that support from the U.S. military would be needed for South Vietnam to have any chance of victory. Kennedy immediately followed up on their recommendation. Around 9,000 U.S. troops were fighting in Vietnam by the middle of 1962. However, the United States had still not officially entered the war between the north and south.

Done with Diem

Buddhist frustration in South Vietnam came to a boil in May 1963. Diem had ordered his Catholic government officials to restrict public displays of religious flags. But an important Buddhist celebration at which flags were usually flown was only days away. Thousands of Buddhists marched in protest. ARVN troops were

Buddhist leaders met with Diem in an effort to improve his treatment of their people.

ordered to fire into the crowd. Nine people were killed in the shootings. Diem tried to shift the blame to Viet Cong guerrillas, but the Buddhists did not believe his excuses. Diem's leadership was quickly unraveling. Buddhist monks protested the shootings by setting themselves ablaze on the streets of Saigon. Television news carried these shocking images around the globe.

Diem had failed to provide the stable government that U.S. leaders had hoped for. Instead, he had become a major political problem for the United States. With Diem's ability to lead his nation through the war in doubt, Kennedy's hand was forced. He agreed to secretly support a military **coup** to remove Diem from power. On November 1, 1963, ARVN forces captured Diem and other top-ranking leaders. Diem was murdered the following day.

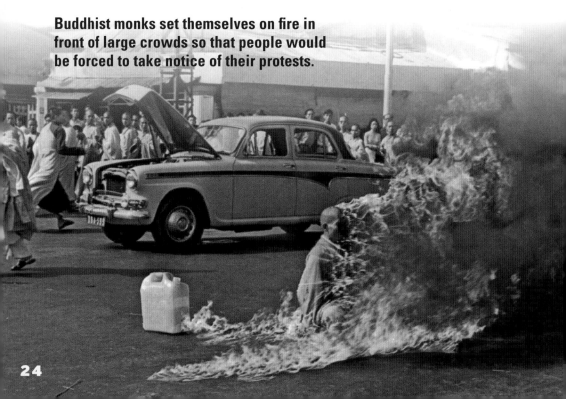

Buddhist monks set themselves on fire in front of large crowds so that people would be forced to take notice of their protests.

The assassination of President Kennedy thrust Lyndon B. Johnson into the spotlight as president.

A committee of South Vietnamese military officials scrambled to set up a temporary government. The Viet Cong seized the opportunity by pushing their attacks even harder. Kennedy hurriedly approved of the new South Vietnamese government on November 8.

Johnson Steps In

President Kennedy was assassinated in Dallas just two weeks after the coup in South Vietnam. Vice President Lyndon Johnson became the nation's president. Johnson kept many of the same foreign policy advisers that Kennedy had relied on. He hoped to continue Kennedy's strategy of keeping U.S. military operations south of the North Vietnamese border. The events of 1964 set him on a different course.

In June, Johnson put General William Westmoreland in command of U.S. forces in Vietnam. Westmoreland favored expanding the war. Five thousand more U.S. troops were sent to Vietnam the following month. This brought the total number of U.S. forces in Vietnam to 21,000.

Tonkin Trouble

In late July, the USS *Maddox* began a **reconnaissance** mission in the Gulf of Tonkin off the coast of North Vietnam. On August 2, the *Maddox* reported that it was under attack from Vietnamese torpedo boats. The U.S. Navy sent a second ship, the *Turner Joy*, to join the *Maddox*. The two ships reported another Vietnamese torpedo attack two days later. However, no

Reports of attacks against the USS *Maddox* drew the United States deeper into the conflict in Vietnam.

North Vietnamese ships were visually confirmed in either reported attack. Despite the lack of evidence, Johnson responded by ordering strikes against North Vietnamese military bases. He announced his decision in a televised address to the American public.

On August 7, Congress granted President Johnson the right to use force to assist South Vietnam in any way that he believed necessary. Johnson did not use his new war powers immediately, though the war had taken a major turn since Diem's removal. The Viet Cong had broadened its influence in South Vietnam. Troops and supplies flowed freely from the north. Worst of all for the United States, none of Diem's successors had been able to establish a stable government or fight insurgents effectively.

President Johnson's televised address to the nation was the first exposure many Americans had to the Gulf of Tonkin incident. His remarks stressed the importance of U.S. involvement in the conflict between North and South Vietnam. Johnson did not mention that the *Maddox* and the *Turner Joy* were on a reconnaissance mission. The address was carefully designed to build support for U.S. involvement in the war.

PRESIDENT JOHNSON'S MESSAGE TO CONGRESS

President Johnson addressed Congress in the wake of the Gulf of Tonkin incident. He stressed the necessity of dealing directly and immediately with communist aggression in Vietnam. See page 60 for a link to read Johnson's message to Congress online.

A Growing Conflict

Johnson steadily moved the United States deeper into the war during the first seven months of 1965. In response to the southward push of the North Vietnamese forces, he approved Operation Rolling Thunder. The operation called for the strategic bombing of dozens of targets in North Vietnam.

U.S. bombers attacked North Vietnamese weapons stores and radars. They also destroyed bridges and

President Johnson signed the Tonkin Gulf Resolution into law on August 7, 1964, giving him the power to wage war in Vietnam.

ferries to cut off supplies from China and the Soviet Union. In March, U.S. ground forces made their first attacks on North Vietnam.

The bombings and ground attacks only inspired the Viet Cong to fight harder. General Westmoreland soon informed President Johnson that a large increase in American combat forces was urgently needed. Johnson responded by sending 100,000 U.S. troops to Vietnam in late July 1965.

The U.S. presence in Vietnam steadily grew over the next two years. Bombing of North Vietnam nearly quadrupled by 1967. By June of that year, the United States had 500,000 troops in Vietnam. With costs growing and the war settling into a **stalemate**, dissatisfaction grew in South Vietnam and the United States.

A VIEW FROM ABROAD

By 1967, the strength of the Viet Cong insurgents had U.S. political and military leaders alike wondering if the war was winnable. From the beginning, U.S. leaders had viewed the war as part of the larger struggle against the spread of communism. The people of Vietnam did not always share this perspective. Many of them waged war to unite their country and gain independence from foreign rule.

CHAPTER 3

WAR FRONTS

Operation Rolling Thunder inflicted massive damage on North Vietnam.

PRESIDENT JOHNSON HAD

hoped in 1965 that Operation Rolling Thunder would bring a quick end to the war. He recognized that ground combat forces were sometimes necessary but tried to delay a full-scale ground war. Instead, U.S. forces mainly fought a tightly controlled air war. Rolling Thunder aircraft had dropped 643,000 tons of bombs on North Vietnam by the end of 1968. These bombings had destroyed nearly three-fifths of the nation's power plants and more than half of its major bridges.

U.S. bombers had to contend with antiaircraft attacks from the North Vietnamese Army.

Hard Targets

Operation Rolling Thunder's gradual buildup gave the North Vietnamese plenty of time to create an air defense system. The Soviets provided radar systems, antiaircraft guns, missiles, and fighter planes. In addition, the North Vietnamese Army (NVA) gave ordinary citizens machine guns to fire at U.S. aircraft. NVA troops used deadly missiles to shoot down U.S. fighters. Some areas were designated by U.S. policy as off-limits for bombing. This left the NVA immune to attacks as they safely placed missile sites and antiaircraft guns in those areas to harass U.S. fighters. Rolling Thunder eventually became an enormous drain on the U.S. economy. By 1966, the

United States paid $9.60 for every dollar of damage the bombs caused in Vietnam.

The NVA and Viet Cong were just as difficult to fight on the ground as they were from the air. They dug secure underground tunnels and used them to store supplies, to travel, and to hide from U.S. troops. They often launched surprise attacks by popping out from hidden holes in the jungle floor and then disappearing back down into the tunnels as quickly as they had appeared.

U.S. forces found it difficult to fight against such methods. Foot soldiers worked tirelessly to flush the Viet Cong out of their hiding places. They flooded tunnels and

A VIEW FROM ABROAD

North Vietnam shared a complex relationship with the Soviet Union. Despite the fact that most Vietnamese wanted unification, the Soviets had supported dividing the country into North and South Vietnam at the 1954 Geneva Conference. In addition, the Soviets had supported the proposal to admit North and South Vietnam to the United Nations as separate nations in 1956. As a result, many North Vietnamese did not trust the Soviets. However, the Soviets were actively supporting the NVA with advanced military technology and training by 1965. Such resources strengthened their fight against South Vietnam and the United States.

dropped explosives down any holes they found. They also sent small, thin soldiers down the holes in an effort to clear out the Viet Cong inside. These soldiers were often called tunnel rats.

U.S. planes dropped chemical **defoliants** to kill plants. This thinned the jungle and made it harder for insurgents to hide in the dense tangles of trees and bushes. Once insurgents were spotted, helicopters equipped with machine guns and grenade launchers sped to battle sites to unload ground forces. Other times, small bands of U.S. troops hiked out to trails used by the Viet Cong, set out land mines, and waited to surprise their enemies.

Viet Cong tunnels had small, hidden entrances that were often difficult to find.

Many South Vietnamese civilians secretly aided the Viet Cong by passing along supplies and information or providing places to hide. As a result, U.S. soldiers rarely trusted any Vietnamese at all. They burned down entire villages when they suspected the locals of harboring the Viet Cong.

Everywhere the Viet Cong became influential, General Westmoreland met them with tremendous force. U.S. troops inflicted heavy **casualties** in many of these attacks but never a knockout blow. The NVA and the Viet Cong seemed to have a never-ending supply of troops. Every year, 200,000 North Vietnamese men reached draft age and replaced their fallen comrades.

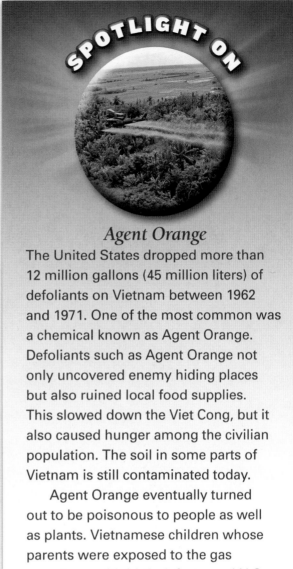

SPOTLIGHT ON

Agent Orange

The United States dropped more than 12 million gallons (45 million liters) of defoliants on Vietnam between 1962 and 1971. One of the most common was a chemical known as Agent Orange. Defoliants such as Agent Orange not only uncovered enemy hiding places but also ruined local food supplies. This slowed down the Viet Cong, but it also caused hunger among the civilian population. The soil in some parts of Vietnam is still contaminated today.

Agent Orange eventually turned out to be poisonous to people as well as plants. Vietnamese children whose parents were exposed to the gas were born with birth defects, and U.S. veterans continue to suffer from cancers caused by Agent Orange exposure.

Martin Luther King Jr. (right) and other war protesters supported boxer Muhammad Ali's (left) opposition to the draft.

Resistance at Home

As the situation grew worse in Vietnam, Americans began to protest the war. In 1966, folksinger Joan Baez encouraged fed-up Americans to refuse to pay taxes used to fund the war. Boxing great Muhammad Ali objected to the war by refusing to serve in the U.S. military when he was **drafted**. By 1967, opposition to the war had increased even more. On April 15, 400,000 protesters rallied at the

A FIRSTHAND LOOK AT
A VIETNAM WAR PROTEST

Millions of Americans did not believe that the U.S. military should continue fighting in the Vietnam War. Many of them expressed their feelings about the war through marches and protests. See page 60 for a link to watch news coverage of one of these marches online.

United Nations in New York City. By July, polls revealed that more and more Americans were beginning to believe that the United States was losing the war.

Draft resistance became more widespread. Protests came to a head at the Lincoln Memorial in Washington, D.C., where 100,000 rallied on October 21. In response to the protests, President Johnson and General Westmoreland

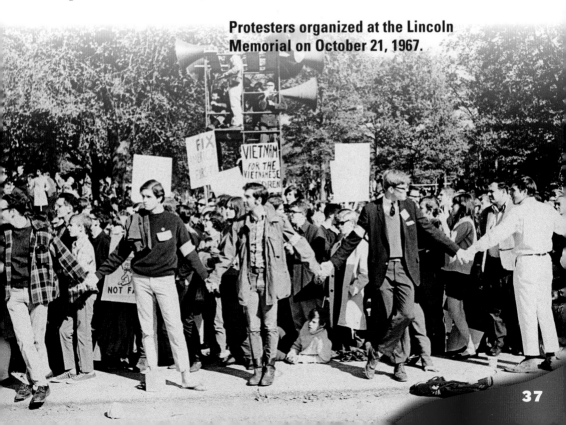

Protesters organized at the Lincoln Memorial on October 21, 1967.

launched a media campaign that aimed to convince U.S. citizens that their country was winning the war. News coverage painted a much different picture. Citizens across the nation began to distrust President Johnson.

Winning Hearts and Minds

At the same time, bombing and search-and-destroy missions were causing massive damage to South Vietnam. Entire villages were destroyed, and the nation's agricultural economy was ruined. Millions of peasants who lost their homes to the attacks fled to refugee camps and into the cities. They grew even more distrustful of the U.S. forces in Vietnam.

Millions of Vietnamese civilians were left homeless because of the damage caused by U.S. forces.

U.S. troops destroyed South Vietnamese villages as they hunted for hidden Viet Cong.

President Johnson believed that winning the hearts and minds of South Vietnam's peasants would discourage support for the Viet Cong. Government programs in agriculture, education, and communications were created. The ARVN encouraged peasants to take part in them. But this did little to break communist resolve in the long run. Distrust between U.S. servicemen and the South Vietnamese occasionally erupted in acts of senseless brutality. The war took a new and dangerous turn at the beginning of 1968.

CHAPTER 4

BRINGING THE WAR HOME

The Tet Offensive increased opposition to the war among U.S. citizens.

IN LATE JANUARY 1968, THE Viet Cong and U.S. forces agreed to a two-day cease-fire during Tet, the Vietnamese New Year celebration. However, the Viet Cong broke the agreement with a series of surprise attacks that came to be known as the Tet Offensive. The Viet Cong launched attacks on more than 100 cities across South Vietnam. Near the border between North and South Vietnam, the Viet Cong overran U.S. forces and occupied the city of Hue for three weeks. They tortured and massacred thousands of Hue residents and U.S. soldiers, burying them in mass graves.

General William Westmoreland believed that the United States could win the war if it increased the number of troops in Vietnam.

Growing War, Growing Problems

The Tet Offensive raised serious doubts in the minds of U.S. citizens that the war was still winnable. Resistance to the war exploded in March when the *New York Times* reported General Westmoreland's request for an additional 206,000 troops. Congress became deeply divided between hawks, supporters of the war, and doves, representatives who opposed it.

The war also threatened the stability of the U.S. economy. By 1967, the cost of the war had surpassed $2 billion per month. High-ranking government officials began to urge Johnson to find a way to negotiate withdrawal from the war. In a televised address on March 31, Johnson announced new restrictions on the bombing of North Vietnam and preliminary plans for withdrawal. He also announced his decision not to run for reelection.

North Vietnam agreed to begin peace talks three days later. But the war was far from over. North Vietnamese leaders pressed their advantage by calling for an end to all bombing and for Viet Cong representatives to be allowed to participate in the peace talks. The United States refused to give in to these demands.

Johnson's actions during the war had made him so unpopular that he chose not to seek reelection.

YESTERDAY'S HEADLINES

Americans were outraged when the NVA and Viet Cong attacked during the Tet cease-fire. What angered them most was the widening gap between what government officials told them about the war and what they saw and read in news reports. The U.S. government claimed that the United States was winning the war. But incidents such as the Tet Offensive showed that the NVA and Viet Cong were well armed and willing to fight. This fueled more antiwar demonstrations.

War protests came back in full force. College and high school students across the United States boycotted classes on April 26. During the Democratic National Convention in August, police riots erupted in Chicago's Grant Park and Lincoln Park when conflict between antiwar protesters and National Guardsmen got out of hand.

The War Rages On

The United States continued to apply tremendous pressure against the insurgents after the Tet Offensive. In 1968 alone, 200,000 communists were killed. In comparison, 14,500 American servicemen were killed. Despite this difference in losses, U.S. forces continued to struggle to gain a decisive advantage. The United States began a new approach to the war with the replacement of General Westmoreland in June 1968. Capture, **interrogation**, and torture of Viet Cong became a priority. U.S. forces also began to hand over more responsibility for the war to the ARVN. U.S. leaders hoped that this would decrease battlefield casualties and protests at home.

By fall, Johnson knew he would have to come to terms with North Vietnamese leaders. Opposition to the war was hurting his party's presidential candidate, Hubert Humphrey, in election polls. In October, Johnson finally agreed to stop all bombing in North Vietnam. In return, he demanded that the NVA limit

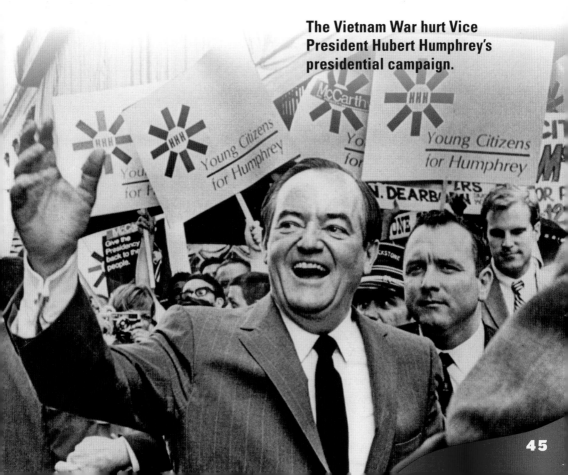

The Vietnam War hurt Vice President Hubert Humphrey's presidential campaign.

Richard Nixon convinced Americans to vote for him by claiming that he had a plan for ending the war.

transport of troops to the south. North Vietnam agreed to these terms. South Vietnamese president Nguyen Van Thieu rejected Johnson's terms after Republican presidential candidate Richard Nixon promised to offer South Vietnam more favorable terms if he was elected. Thieu pulled out of the peace talks three days before the U.S. presidential election. Nixon beat Humphrey in the November election by less than 1 percent of the vote. The war continued.

Nixon Takes Over

Nixon had campaigned on the promise that he had a secret plan to end the war quickly. It soon became apparent that Nixon did not have such a plan, but he did take a different approach. With the help of National Security Adviser Henry Kissinger, he worked to improve relations with the Soviet Union and China. Nixon hoped to eliminate their support for North Vietnam. At the same time, he increased bombing of North Vietnam and reduced the number of U.S. ground forces.

Nixon continued the gradual

YESTERDAY'S HEADLINES

U.S. protests against the war exploded in November 1969 when journalist Seymour Hersh (above) reported on the cover-up of a massacre in My Lai, South Vietnam. U.S. troops had suspected the My Lai villagers of harboring Viet Cong. In their search for the Viet Cong, U.S. soldiers murdered hundreds of unarmed people.

When news of the My Lai massacre broke 20 months after the event, Americans were outraged by the cover-up and horrified by the images appearing in the news. One color photograph of dead women and children became a well-known poster that served to energize the antiwar protest.

withdrawal of U.S. ground troops. But this did little to encourage peace talks. In April 1970, he decided that invading Cambodia might disrupt communist supply lines and pressure North Vietnamese leaders into peace. The plan backfired. Viewed as an unprovoked attack on a neutral country, the invasion of Cambodia caused students on campuses across the United States to rise in protest.

On May 4, National Guardsmen called in for crowd control at Ohio's Kent State University fired 67 shots at the unarmed protesters. The shots killed four students and paralyzed another. The nation reeled in horror. A week later, 100,000 demonstrators rallied at the Lincoln Memorial in Washington, D.C. Police surrounded the White House with buses to keep protesters at bay. Protests

People across the country were outraged by the Kent State shootings.

closed high schools and colleges across the nation. In New York City, hundreds of construction workers grew fed up with nearby protesters and attacked them. America seemed to be coming apart at the seams.

Plans for Peace

Split between hawks and doves, Congress reversed the 1964 Tonkin Gulf Resolution. This restricted Nixon's ability to press the war. He responded by withdrawing ground forces from Cambodia and reducing U.S. troops in South Vietnam. By late 1971, just more than 150,000 U.S. troops remained in Vietnam. Encouraged, the Viet Cong went on the offensive in March 1972. Nixon answered by stepping up air attacks and ordering a naval **blockade** of North Vietnamese ports.

In late 1972, the United States and North Vietnam began a new round of peace negotiations in Paris, France. Nguyen Van Thieu was unhappy with the terms that U.S. and North Vietnamese leaders agreed on, as they allowed NVA troops to remain in South Vietnam. Despite Thieu's objections, the negotiations moved forward and a final agreement was reached on January 27, 1973. The U.S.

Vice President Gerald Ford took over as president when Richard Nixon was forced out of office.

military draft was ended the same day. U.S. forces soon began heading home from Vietnam. On March 29, the last official U.S. combat forces left Vietnam. However, about 8,500 "civilian technicians" were left behind in support positions with the ARVN. They continued to help the ARVN fight North Vietnamese communists even though the United States had agreed to a cease-fire.

The United States continued to pump aid into the war effort, but it was all for nothing. President Nixon was caught up in an unrelated scandal. He resigned as president on August 9, 1974, and was replaced by Vice President Gerald Ford. Ford was turned down when he asked Congress to approve aid to Vietnam. The NVA and Viet Cong insurgents now pressed forward against minimal resistance. On April 21, 1975, with the capture of Saigon unavoidable, President Thieu resigned.

On April 29, the NVA began moving swiftly across Saigon. Desperate South Vietnamese civilians swarmed the U.S. Embassy in Saigon. The United States had a plan in place for helicopter evacuations. By 2:00 p.m. local time, evacuations had begun. The frantic airlift to U.S. Navy ships continued into the next day. Nearly 7,000 Vietnamese and Americans had been lifted to safety by the time Saigon fell.

Televised coverage followed the evacuation minute by minute. As the last helicopter carried Vietnamese citizens to safety, America's long nightmare finally reached an end. After the cost of 58,178 American lives and $111 billion, the United States had lost the Vietnam War.

South Vietnamese citizens relied on U.S. forces during the evacuation from Saigon.

CHINA

NORTH VIETNAM

Hanoi

Hanoi
During the Vietnam War, the city of Hanoi was the capital of North Vietnam. It continued to be the capital of Vietnam after reunification.

LAOS

Gulf of Tonkin

THAILAND

My Lai

SOUTH VIETNAM

CAMBODIA

Saigon
Saigon is the largest city in Vietnam. During the war, it was the capital of South Vietnam. It is known today as Ho Chi Minh City.

Saigon

MAP OF THE EVENTS

What Happened Where?

Gulf of Tonkin

In early August 1964, two U.S. ships in the Gulf of Tonkin reported unprovoked attacks from North Vietnamese torpedoes. The incident drew the United States closer to all-out war against North Vietnam.

South China Sea

My Lai

On March 16, 1968, U.S. soldiers killed hundreds of unarmed Vietnamese civilians during a search for hidden Viet Cong in the village of My Lai. When the incident was revealed in the American media, it caused an increase in protests against the war.

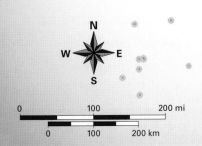

0   100   200 mi

0   100   200 km

Healing Old Wounds

President Bill Clinton, with President Tran Duc Luong, helped heal the divide between the United States and Vietnam.

On July 2, 1976, North and South Vietnam were brought together under communist rule. For two decades, the United States severed all ties with the newly unified nation. Beginning in 1995, President Bill Clinton worked to reestablish normal relations with Vietnam. Since then, the two nations have established trade, and the U.S. government has invested heavily in Vietnam. Many private U.S. companies have also developed direct relations with Vietnam.

In 2007, political leaders and scientists from the two nations opened discussions about the impact of Agent Orange on Vietnam. Plans to clean up the remaining poison have been put in place. The United States has also spearheaded efforts to assist Vietnamese who were disabled by the harmful chemicals used during the war. The wounds of Vietnam, many and deep, have begun to heal. The war may finally be coming to an end.

Workers are still attempting to erase the effects of Agent Orange on Vietnam.

Ho Chi Minh

Lyndon B. Johnson

Ho Chi Minh (1890–1969) was a Vietnamese revolutionary who served as president of North Vietnam until his death.

Ngo Dinh Diem (1901–1963) was president of South Vietnam from 1955 to 1963. He alienated his country's Buddhist majority and was assassinated after being forced from office.

Lyndon B. Johnson (1908–1973) was the 36th president of the United States. He greatly expanded the U.S. military presence in Vietnam, causing widespread protests in America.

Richard M. Nixon (1913–1994) was the 37th president of the United States. He recognized the necessity of drawing down ground forces in Vietnam. He became the only U.S. president to date to resign from office, following an unrelated scandal.

William Westmoreland (1914–2005) was the commander of U.S. military operations in Vietnam from 1964 to 1968. He was a chief architect of the Rolling Thunder air strikes and believed that the United States could win in Vietnam by wearing down its enemies over time.

William Westmoreland

Henry Kissinger (1923–) was the national security adviser and later secretary of state under Richard Nixon. He was awarded the Nobel Peace Prize in 1973 for his efforts in negotiating the end of the Vietnam War.

Nguyen Van Thieu (1923–2001) became leader of South Vietnam in 1965. He served as president from 1967 to 1975. He was accused of appointing personal favorites rather than competent leaders in the ARVN.

TIMELINE

1950

February
The United States supports the French military in Vietnam.

August
Truman sends the first U.S. military advisers to Vietnam.

1954

May
North Vietnam defeats the French at Dien Bien Phu.

July 21
The Geneva Conference splits Vietnam into two separate nations.

1964

June
General William Westmoreland is placed in control of U.S. military forces in Vietnam.

August
The Gulf of Tonkin incident draws the United States into the war officially.

1965

Operation Rolling Thunder begins.

1970

May 4
National Guardsmen shoot and kill protesters at Kent State University.

1971

U.S. troops begin withdrawing from Vietnam.

1961

President Kennedy sends U.S. special forces to Vietnam.

1963

November 2
South Vietnamese President Ngo Dinh Diem is assassinated.

1968

The Tet Offensive touches off widespread protests in the United States.

1969

November
News of the My Lai massacre breaks in the United States.

1973

The U.S. military draft is terminated.

1975

April 21
South Vietnamese President Nguyen Van Thieu resigns.

1976

July 2
North and South Vietnam are unified under communist rule.

LIVING HISTORY

Primary sources provide firsthand evidence about a topic. Witnesses to a historical event create primary sources. They include autobiographies, newspaper reports of the time, oral histories, photographs, and memoirs. A secondary source analyzes primary sources, and is one step or more removed from the event. Secondary sources include textbooks, encyclopedias, and commentaries. To view the following primary and secondary sources, go to www.factsfornow.scholastic.com. Enter the keywords **Vietnam War** and look for the Living History logo Σ¡.

Σ¡ **The Final Declaration of the Geneva Conference** The Geneva Conference divided Vietnam into two separate nations. It also worked to end hostilities in Cambodia and Laos.

Σ¡ **The Kent State Shootings** John Filo's Pulitzer Prize–winning photograph of the aftermath of the Kent State shootings captured the emotional impact of the war and the terrible price paid by Americans who stood up for their beliefs.

Σ¡ **President Johnson's Message to Congress** President Johnson addressed Congress in the wake of the Gulf of Tonkin incident. He stressed the necessity of dealing directly and immediately with communist aggression in Vietnam.

Σ¡ **A Vietnam War Protest** Millions of Americans did not believe that the U.S. military should continue fighting in the Vietnam War. Many of them expressed their feelings about the war through marches and protests.

RESOURCES

Books

Caputo, Philip. *10,000 Days of Thunder: A History of the Vietnam War.* New York: Atheneum Books for Young Readers, 2005.

Kent, Deborah. *The Vietnam War: From Da Nang to Saigon.* Berkeley Heights, NJ: Enslow, 2011.

Murray, Stuart. *Vietnam War.* New York: DK Publishing, 2005.

Perritano, John. *Vietnam War.* New York: Franklin Watts, 2010.

Visit this Scholastic Web site for more information on the Vietnam War:
www.factsfornow.scholastic.com
Enter the keywords **Vietnam War**

GLOSSARY

blockade (blok-ADE) the closing off of an area, such as a port, to keep people or supplies from going in or out

casualties (KAZH-oo-uhl-teez) people killed or wounded during warfare

communist (KAHM-yuh-nist) someone who follows the philosophy that all the land, property, business, and resources belong to the government or community and that the profits should be shared by all

coup (KOO) a sudden and highly successful act

defoliants (dee-FOH-lee-uhnts) chemical sprays or dusts applied to plants in order to cause the leaves to drop off

drafted (DRAF-tid) selected for a purpose, such as to join the armed forces

economic (ek-uh-NAH-mik) of or having to do with the system of buying, selling, and making things in a place

insurgents (in-SUR-jints) people who are attempting to overthrow an established government

interrogation (in-ter-uh-GAY-shuhn) detailed questioning, usually in connection with a crime

nationalist (NASH-uh-nuh-list) someone who is very proud of his or her country or who wants it to be independent

reconnaissance (rih-KAHN-uh-suhns) activities used to gain knowledge of enemy plans or tactics

siege (SEEJ) the surrounding of a place, such as a city, to cut off supplies and then wait for the people inside to surrender

stalemate (STALE-mate) a position or situation that results in a deadlock, with no progress possible

unify (YOO-nuh-fye) to bring or join together into a whole; to unite

INDEX

Page numbers in *italics* indicate illustrations.

ABOUT THE AUTHOR

Peter Benoit is a graduate of Skidmore College in Saratoga Springs, New York. His degree is in mathematics. He is the author of dozens of books with Children's Press and has written on topics as diverse as Native Americans, ecosystems, disasters, American history, and ancient civilizations. Peter has also written more than 2,000 poems. He lives in Greenwich, New York.